The Secret Jewish Law of Attraction

Using the Law of Attraction to Attract your Goals, Desires, and Dreams

D1462228

By Rabbi Haim Abraham

Introduction

The Talmud in Tracate Makot page 10 says "in the way which man want to go, so he is led." Rabbi Shmuel Eidels (1555 – 1631), a renowned rabbi and Talmudist explained this to mean that each time a person has a thought about what they want to do, have, or be in life, they create an angle from that thought that then leads them on that path. Talk about the law of attraction!

Whether you're Jewish or not, there is much to be learned from the Jewish texts about the law of attraction. Based on ancient books, such as the Talmud and Kabbala, as well as even older books such as the Torah, this book provides you with the most important concepts that emerge from the ancient truths of Judaism. This is not a religious book; you don't need to start practicing any religious rituals, or say any prayers, although of course, you can if you'd like.

The Jewish Law of Attraction breaks up into two parts. One, is how to get or attract a specific thing you want. This requires understanding how to set intentions and how to ask for what it is you want. The second and much more beneficial part and we will start this book off with this part, is how to raise your energy levels so that good things are naturally attracted to you, as well as repelling any negative events in life. This requires a much deeper, inner change, but is also much more beneficial in both the short and long term.

This book is the product of many years of study. This book boils it down to easy to understand concepts, as well as easy to apply exercises and mindsets.

You will learn some fairly simple ideas, but don't let that fool you; their effectiveness has been proven over and over, from generation from generation. These are powerful tools that when used on a consistent basis will provide you with natural law of attraction powers and strength.

I'd also like to point out an issue I've become aware of lately. There are religious sects that subscribe to the idea of the "prosperity gospel," meaning that if one lives a righteous life and performs good deeds they will be rewarded in this life, in this world, with wealth and opulence. This is not a Jewish concept. As the Mishna says in Avot (4:2), the reward of a Mitzvah is another Mitzvah. The word Mitzvah literally means commandment, but it is also used to explain good deeds. So, what the Mishna is telling us is that the reward for fulling a mitzvah is getting the chance to do another mitzvah. That is because the reward for even a single mitzvah is too large to even bestow us with it in this world. The only way to reward someone for a mitzvah therefore is to provide them with another opportunity to perform a Mitzvah.

Rather, the basic Jewish concept about how to achieve wealth is not about performing good deeds, although that is not to say that one shouldn't perform good deeds. Just don't perform good deeds (except for tithing, more on that later), with the expectation that it will bring you wealth. That's not the point of good deeds. Good deeds need to be performed with a pure heart, not in order to get something in return. Rather, the basic idea of Jewish philosophy on how to become wealthy is being honest in business, prayer, believing in G-d, raising one's positive energy or luck, and G-d's grace. Of course, we will cover all of these ideas and more in the book. On the other side, when one does evil, that is a barrier to success, at least in the long term. I will explain in more detail this idea in the book later on.

You are created in His Image, therefore, you are a creator. You create with your mind. You prepare the tools to accept your desires with your actions. You enhance your mind with kindness. You enhance your tools with peace. A short powerful prayer: G-d, the good bring close, the bad make distant, and the good in Your eyes fulfill.

Lastly, before we start, I do offer to take your requests and pray for you, meditate for your request, and apply my law of attraction to attract you your desires. If you are interested, please email me at **rabbiabrahamloa@gmail.com**.

Part One

Chapter One Think Good

As mentioned in the introduction, we are going to start with the more general techniques, those that help raise our energy levels and thus start creating on auto mode.

There's an old Hasidic saying, from the dynasty of Lubavitch, "Tracht gut, vet zein gut," meaning "think good, and it will be good." Doesn't get more law of attraction than that! And it's true, when you think good it will be good.

But it gets deeper.

There is an amazing story in the Talmud, about Rabbi Yohanan. As he was walking with his students, they came across a cow carcass. His students remarked about what foul smell the carcass had, to which the Rabbi replied, "yes, but look how white its teeth are!" In other words, seeing the good in even a smelly dead cow will bring out the good in life. As Rabbi Nachman from Breslev teaches us, when we favorably judge others, we actually can cause the good to arouse in people. Even when someone is not on the right path, if we judge them favorably and love them, they may indeed be inspired to return to the righteous path.

See the good in people, situations, and of course in yourself. And as the Hasidic saying promises, it will then be good.

Here's two more things that will enhance this seemingly simple concept of thinking good. For one, set an intention. Simply say "I am setting the intention that," fill in the blank. Then, believe that it will happen, that it will work out, that it will be in your best interest.

But what to do when you don't have any specific intention you want to set? Or in a situation where you feel overwhelmed, too stressed out to set a specific intention? In that case, simply think the word "good." Just hold that one word in your mind as a way of setting an intention.

While this may sound simplistic, it can be a powerful technique. You can also use this technique with different words. Hold the word "wealth," or "love," or "happiness" in your head. You really don't need anything more than that. Holding the words in your head set the intention, and begin the process of creating angels that work to bring you your desire.

In Genesis it says that G-d created us in His image. But Judaism teaches that G-d has no image; what image, then, are we created in? The answer is simple, He created us in His image as it relates to His creation of us, meaning, as creators. We are not G-ds, but we have the power to create, to some extent, as G-d does. This is important to remember; you can create more wealth in your life, more happiness, more love. You can solve problems on a universal level. Just think good, and it will indeed be good.

You are created in His Image, therefore, you are a creator. You create with your mind. You prepare the tools to accept your desires with your actions. You enhance your mind with kindness. You enhance your tools with peace. A short powerful prayer: G-d, the good bring close, the bad make distant, and the good in Your eyes fulfill.

Chapter Two Worrying

The Talmud in Tractate Horayoth teaches us that worrying lessons one luck. In the law of attraction terms, worrying is, by definition, thinking about all the things that can go wrong. This lessons one's luck, or energy, making us vulnerable.

Of course, the question then, what can one do in order to not worry? For one, catch yourself right away when you start worrying. As soon as you do, use the technique from chapter one and just think the word "good," or a variation of it. That will really help to end the spiral of the downward thinking. Good! It will be good!

Once you've come out of the spiral, you must take your thoughts in the opposite direction. Start thinking not just good, but great thoughts! Whatever it was you were worrying about, start imagining what you it would be like if not just did the specific issue work out, but it turns out even better than you had previously imagined! Were you worrying about money? Stop the spiral by thinking just that one word, "good," and then start imagining what it will be like when you not just don't have to worry about money, but that you have a huge abundance of it! This of course can be applied to any issue you may be having.

Worrying sends a message that you don't trust that everything will be okay. Worrying suggests that you lack belief. But, worrying can also cause you to take action. If you are worried about not being able to find a job, you will send out more resumes. If you are worried about not finding love, you will go out on more dates. So, how can we make sure we take advantage of worrying without suffering the detriments? Very simple: As the Ramchal, a prominent Italian Jewish rabbi, kabbalist, and philosopher (1707-1746) teaches, your prosperity doesn't come *from* your work, it comes *through* your work. The difference is simple.

Think of an ATM. Your money doesn't come from the ATM; the ATM doesn't provide you money in the sense that you provide it value and in exchange it pays you. But, your money does come through it. Another example would be a window, where someone hands you your dinner through the window. Your dinner doesn't come from the dinner, it is just channeled through it.

So, when worrying causes you to apply to more jobs, or to ask your boss for a raise, or to start your own company, you need to keep in mind that you are only worried about creating an ATM or a window, where prosperity can be given to you through it, but that the actual source of your wealth and abundance is from G-d.

It stands to reason that if worrying lessons one luck, trusting will raise it. I touch on this in a later chapter in much more depth.

You are created in His Image, therefore, you are a creator. You create with your mind. You prepare the tools to accept your desires with your actions. You enhance your mind with kindness. You enhance your tools with peace. A short powerful prayer: G-d, the good bring close, the bad make distant, and the good in Your eyes fulfill.

Chapter Three Be Specific

There is a great story of a man who came to his Rabbi with a problem. "Rabbi," he said, "I have brainstormed for days and came up with 100 ways in which G-d could solve my problem." The Rabbi heard some of the options, and said "I wouldn't be surprised if your solution is the 101 option you haven't thought of." And indeed it was.

What this story illustrates is that when trying to achieve a specific goal, don't worry about the "how." The "how" is for G-d, not for us to figure out. This will help with what we spoke about in the previous chapter, about not worrying. Now that you know that you need only focus on the "what," but not on the "how," you need not worry, at least not as much.

Well, in that case, you might ask, if I'm not worrying about the how, should I even take any action at all to achieve my goal? Of course you do. Again, this goes back to the previous chapter, as far as making the ATM, the window, in other words the tool, that is there to help you achieve your goal.

In other words, as long as you are making some effort to achieve a goal, such as applying to jobs or going on some dates, you've thus created the tool *through* which G-d will deliver your goal. It may turn out to be something completely different, come from a completely different direction, be that 101th solution, but this way you can achieve your goal *and* be worry free.

On the other hand, you do want to be very specific when stating your intention. By the way, I will cover in a later chapter the best ways to state your intention, including how and even where you should do so.

There is a story in the Talmud of a Rabbi who was stranded in the desert and began the long journey home on foot. He prayed simply for a donkey, without specifying what he needed the donkey for. Lo and behold, a Roman general passes by, with his soldiers and his own donkeys. One of the donkeys had become sick, so when he saw the rabbi, he forced him to carry the donkey the rest of the way. Moral of the story: be specific!

Being specific doesn't mean you need to give every small detail of your request. If you want to find a new house to buy or rent, you don't need to specify every room and closet you are looking for. Simply stating that you want to find a home for sale that will provide you the best you can afford. What wouldn't be considered specific is something like asking for a home. A home for rent, or for purchase, is much more specific and should do the trick.

In summary, don't worry, be happy!

Chapter Four Gossiping Poison

Another huge drain on your energy levels is gossiping. Gossiping, in Jewish traditional teachings, can actually transfer to the person being gossiped about the merit of our own good deeds and positive energy.

Gossiping does not apply when you're trying to warn a friend or family member about a potential scam, bad person, etc., or when talking to a therapist, and other essential needs to talk.

The gossiping I'm referring to hear is the quintessential two friends talking about a third "friend" about what he or she wore to work that day, who they started dating, and so on. Just the pointless waste of energy where no good comes out of it. But don't think of the damage it causes as just a simple everyday type thing. You are literally draining your energy, whether or not the other person gets your energy doesn't matter. Bottom line is that is detrimental to you and really provides no benefits at all.

On that note, there are indeed other bad acts that can drain our energy. No bad act is ever beneficial; the reason I brought up gossiping is become it can seem quite harmless when in fact it's quite the opposite.

You might ask, as many do, how can you avoid gossip, when you are talking with a friend on the phone and they start talking about something you'd like to avoid? Here's what I've learned. When you tell people that you don't gossip, people respect that. In a way, you are appealing to their higher selves, and many people will live up to higher expectations when challenged. This may seem hard at first, but it will get easier, and the benefits will quickly become obvious.

You are created in His Image, therefore, you are a creator. You create with your mind. You prepare the tools to accept your desires with your actions. You enhance your mind with kindness. You enhance your tools with peace. A short powerful prayer: G-d, the good bring close, the bad make distant, and the good in Your eyes fulfill.

Chapter Five Money is Good

When the Torah tells us about Abraham, it goes into great detail about how much money he had, how many cattle and sheep he had, and so on. It also tells us about other very spiritual men and how wealthy they were. Why does this matter? What is the lesson?

The lesson is that wealth is good, and not anti-spiritual, as some other philosophers teach. It matters because not just is it not anti-spiritual, it actually helps one achieve a higher spiritual state.

When it comes to the law of attraction, it is important to understand that wealth is a good thing, and to not come from a place of lack and limitation. If you subconsciously believe that wealth is a bad thing, it will be very difficult to attract it.

So, how does one know when they have these subconscious beliefs? One simple way is to look at your bank account. If you don't have enough money there as you'd like, chances are you have some subconscious beliefs that are keeping you there.

As I mentioned in the introduction, in the way one wants to go, he or she is so led. The way a person "wants" to go, would seem to mean what they *really* want, i.e. what their subconscious wants.

Of course, the next question is then how does one change their deep, subconscious beliefs? If you've read other law of attraction books, this question is tackled from all sorts of angles. Being politically correct, most books don't want to really tell you the best way to do this, because the absolute best way to this is through prayer. As King David says in the Psalms, G-d knows man's deepest thoughts. Only He can really know what's inside in the deepest realms of your mind. And, it would follow, only He knows how to change them.

Praying is easy. All you need to do is say "G-d, please help me with..." fill in the blank. If you really want to learn the most powerful prayer techniques, I would recommend reading a book called "Gates of Prayer," by Rabbi Shimshon Pincus. He advances the ten techniques taught in Jewish tradition.

While there are other legitimate techniques being taught out there for clearing these subconscious limiting beliefs, such as EFT, Jewish philosophy is that prayer is the most powerful tool. As the story goes, a Rabbi asks one of his students what happened to his hand, as it was bandaged up and clearly inured. The man replied that he was using a hammer and accidentally hit his finger while completing a task at home. "Well then," said the Rabbi, "you must have not prayed hard enough before the task."

The lesson being of course that prayer can and should be used on everything. How much more so on discovering and releasing hidden subconscious beliefs!

Speaking of Abraham, there is a story about him in the book of Genesis, about how he prayed for the wellbeing of Avshalom, and that he be healed. In response, G-d healed Abraham and his wife Sarah, and they were then able to conceive and have a child, Isaac. The sages teach that this means that when a person prays for someone else, the one offering the prayer is answered first.

This is an amazing prayer technique! Simply pray for someone else with the same issue you may be having. You can even offer a close friend or family member to pray for each other, knowing that it will strengthen both prayers.

Chapter Six – Gratitude

Gratitude is a common theme in Judaism. When Moses was going to turn the Nile River into blood, as commanded by G-d, he asked his older brother, Aaron, to do so, because Moses had gratitude towards the Nile for saving him as a baby. The sages teach that if Moses was grateful towards an inanimate object, the Nile, how much more so must we be grateful towards G-d and people for the kindness they bestow us with daily. There was a rabbi a generation or two ago who would wear his shoes until they were simply unwearable, and then buy a new pair. He would then rap the old pair in newspaper before throwing them away, to show his gratitude to the shoes.

There are other examples in the Torah of this, but the point is that gratitude must be something we not just feel, but actually do. While feeling grateful is good, we need to show our gratitude through action.

Saying "thank you" is indeed the first step. And many times, that it all we need. Thank the barista for your coffee. Thank the mailman for your mail.

But often, we need to go a little bit further. Can you tip the barista? Can you get the mailman a "happy holidays" card, or offer him a cup of cold water on a hot day?

Thank G-d for any and all senses you possess. Thank G-d for your talents, for your desire to learn and become a better person, and for your abundance in life. To make the point a bit stronger, donate to a charity that feeds the poor, as this not only shows your gratitude but it also makes peace between the poor individual receiving the charity and G-d. Many people, understandably so, are angry with G-d when they are hungry. The Midrash says that when you give charity you make peace between those that are indeed angry and G-d. That is huge!

Here's an even higher level of gratitude. Helping those who don't show their appreciation. When you try and help someone and they don't show their appreciation, the gut reaction is to then stop helping this person. But if you can show G-dly consciousness and continue to help someone despite their lack of gratitude, you raise your energy to very high levels. This may actually be an uncommon event, but if it does happen, seize the opportunity!

On a similar note, the Talmud says that one who holds their tongue during a fight and doesn't respond when they know they can, at that moment, the whole world sits on their shoulders. This is not in the case of a false accusation, though. If someone accuses you of shoplifting, you shouldn't just stand there and not say anything, of course. This is in a case of a "normal" fight, such as the ones we have with family and spouses, or even with friends. If you can refrain from answering and thereby stop the fight, you raise your energy to the highest levels possible.

I heard a reliable story about a man and wife who were trying for many years to have a baby. One day, the husband was witness to a quarrel where one person highly provoked another person. The husband rushed up to the second person, and begged him to go outside with him for just a moment. He explained that him and his wife were trying to have a child and that if he would agree not to answer anything back to the provocateur, would he please keep in mind that it would be to the merit of the couple and that they would therefore merit a baby. The man agreed, and, miraculously, nine months later, they had a baby boy.

As you may have already notices, a lot of Jewish law of attraction and thus this book is about raising your energy in general. This is because it's not enough to focus on a specific goal or desire and work on obtaining it. It is much more efficient to raise your core energy and then when there is something you are trying to achieve it will prove much easier.

Lastly on the topic of gratitude, let me just reiterate why it's so important and beneficial to show one's appreciation by giving to charity or helping others. Simply put, the more people you can cause to feel gratitude, the more gratitude you are releasing to the Universe or to G-d. If you donate a Thanksgiving dinner to a family of five, you now have helped all those five people feel gratitude, which is much more powerful than feeling gratitude just on your own.

Chapter Seven – Relationships with Other People

Jewish texts are full of laws, customs, stories and more about the relationship between people. More than half, six to be exact, of the ten commandments are about them. Don't kill, don't covet, respect your parents, and so on. When it comes to the law of attraction and raising your core energy, one must be extra careful about what we do to cause others to feel good or bad. We dedicated a whole chapter to gossip, but of course there are plenty of other things we need to be careful about. Gossip got its own chapter because many people think that "what someone doesn't know won't hurt them," but that is simply not the case.

I think we all know what it means to be careful about treating others fairly, so I'm not going to go into that. I will however share a story that shows just how important it is.

The story is from the Talmud Ketubot 62b. It is told of Rabbi Rehumi who was a Torah scholar and would study all year in Yeshiva, away from home. He would come home only once a year, on Yom Kippur, to see his wife. One year, he was so engaged in Toray study that he forgot to go home. His wife waited at home and once she realized he wasn't coming home, she started to cry. Instantly, the roof fell in and killed the Rabbi. Now let me just say, before going any further, that the rabbi was at a very high spiritual level and thus punishment came much faster.

Rabbi Haim Schmulevitz, from Jerusalem, Israel, asked the following question: Why did G-d punish Rabbi Rehumi by killing him, since that was the last thing his wife would have wanted? The answer is that when dealing with the relationship between people, we are dealing with fire. When a fire breaks out in a building, the fire doesn't care who is a good person or who is a bad person, it simply burns everything in its path. That's how careful we need to be with how we treat others.

That being said, we should also be liberal when it comes to forgiveness. Holding a grudge against others is not a good idea. You can forgive someone without ever telling them, and without ever seeing them again. But it is also very beneficial to you to forgive others.

In Jewish tradition, we recite a small prayer every night and the first part of it is about forgiving others. We say that we forgive people for any transgression they made against us that day, or any other day, in this life or in a previous life, whether the person hurt us purposely or by accident, etc.

Forgiveness is also a great way to raise your energy levels. It releases energy that is going to holding the grudge. Now that you've let go of the grudge, you can now benefit from that energy!

In summary, do your absolute best to treat others with dignity. As the Torah says in Leviticus, "love your fellow person like you love yourself."

You are created in His Image, therefore, you are a creator. You create with your mind. You prepare the tools to accept your desires with your actions. You enhance your mind with kindness. You enhance your tools with peace. A short powerful prayer: G-d, the good bring close, the bad make distant, and the good in Your eyes fulfill.

Chapter Eight Stress is cumulative – Kabbala Breathing Exercise

Stress is one of the worse things a person can allow themselves to accumulate. And I use the word "accumulate" deliberately, because stress is indeed cumulative. It's not enough to release stress on an annual or bi-annual trip. Stress needs to be released on a daily basis, even twice a day.

I'd like to offer you a breathing exercise based on Kabbala that will do wonders to help you release stress. If done consistently, this exercise will yield very positive results. The key is that it is done long term though. At first, the exercise will release stress from your day, but after about a week or so it will continue to release your daily stress plus stress from the past.

The exercise is based on the four levels of creation, as defined in Kabbala, as well as on the Jewish significance of the number 10. So, sit up straight but without feeling to uptight, or lie down. Close your eyes and turn off your phone and do your best to eliminate any distractions. This exercise won't take longer than a couple of minutes.

Now, close your eyes. Breathe in for four seconds, one, two, three, four, then hold your breath for four seconds. Now exhale for four seconds, and then hold on empty for four seconds. Then inhale again for four seconds as you repeat this 10 times.

This should take exactly two minutes and forty seconds. Not bad for such a strong exercise that can have such positive benefits.

Do this exercise, twice a day. After a week or so try to increase to four times a day if you can. Like with other chapters in this book, specially in Part One, this will raise your energy levels and you'll have a much easier time attracting your desires.

Chapter 9 Fasting

A very powerful way in Jewish philosophy to raise your energy and attain a specific goal or desire is fasting. Traditionally, this meant going without food from sunrise to sunset. Although there are the set fast days, many kabbalists and even laymen would fast with a specific goal in mind. Before you embark on any change to your diet, especially something as drastic as going without food and drink for a full day, please consult with your doctor. Fasting is not for everyone, but now we'll discuss ways you can fast without refraining from food and drink.

There is another way you can fast that will yield powerful results as well. Many Kabbalists would recommend going on a "talking fast," where you don't talk for a day or even for just a few hours. The idea of this is twofold. First, you are giving up something, something you usually have a materialistic enjoyment from. Second, and perhaps the better reason, is that by refraining from speech for a day you are also refraining from gossip, bad language, insulting others, and so on.

Today, it is recommended to use more modern fasts. For example, you can go on a "phone fast," where you don't use your phone for a specific number of hours or even for a whole day. You can go on a social media fast for a day or more, on a "news" fast, on a television fast, or even on an internet fast. Although there a lot of positive, productive uses for all of these, they can also be used to waste time, to consume trashy material and gossip, and so on. So, giving them up for even half of a day will have a positive effect on you.

So, while these fasts can be done for your general benefit or the general benefit of your family or even for the world, you can also do them with a specific intent in mind. Now while I say "in mind," really you should state your intention out loud. Very simply, either before or after the fast or both, simply say I will go on a (fill in the blank) fast with the intention that I will (fill in the blank) or may the merit of the (fill in the blank) fast that I just completed may I merit (fill in the blank).

Lastly, you can also go on a sweet or junk food fast, where you don't eat any sort of "treats," such as cookies, ice cream, pizza, soda, and so on. Basically anything that is not just a healthy simple food, even if it tastes great. Eating a pizza rather than a healthy salad, chicken with quinoa, and mineral water, is definitely not in the service of your body and therefore of G-d. Therefore, giving it up for a day or a week, does show G-d that you are giving up something you enjoy for Him, and He will be more likely to then fulfill your desires.

As it says in Pirkey Avot, "Make His [G-d's] will like your will, so that He will make your will like His will. Nullify your will to His will, so that He will nullify the will of others to your will."

In summary, fasting is a powerful way to beseech help from above, but fasting does not have to be a food and drink fast. Going on a social media fast, a television fast, and so on, can be just as effective.

You are created in His Image, therefore, you are a creator. You create with your mind. You prepare the tools to accept your desires with your actions. You enhance your mind with kindness. You enhance your tools with peace. A short powerful prayer: G-d, the good bring close, the bad make distant, and the good in Your eyes fulfill.

Chapter 10 Trusting G-d

Here is a short idea about trusting in G-d, and how the trust itself is meritorious, and thus provides us with abundance:

The common perception of this concept is that we trust in G-d that whatever happens to us will be good. That is, we believe G-d is good, and that whatever endeavor we undertake and any situation we find ourselves in, then because G-d is good, things will be good.

Of course, there are two possible outcomes. Either the event will turn out good, or it won't. So what happened? The usual explanation is that it depends on whether we are worthy or not. That is, if we merit it, then it will be for the good, if not, then it won't be for the good.

Now, even those who explain trusting G-d this way, will qualify things slightly. If a bad occurrence happens, then true, it is a bad occurrence to us. On the revealed plane to us, this appears bad. However, on the hidden level it is all good. Everything that occurs to us G-d intends for our good. At a particular time, an event might appear to us to be bad, however, the inner intent is for our good. Sometimes, after the passage of time this inner goodness in the event will become apparent to us, and sometimes it might never become revealed. Still, our Trust in G-d is that G-d is good and that we believe even the revealed bad contains within it a deeper inner good (just not perceivable by human-kind).

There is a quote from Chovat Levavot. We must trust in G-d, the One who grants good to those who deserve AND to those who do not deserve.

Prayer and repentance have the ability to change our situation. Through repentance we become meritorious. Though before we were not deserving of a certain thing, through repentance we transform ourselves.

The same is through Trust. By trusting in G-d, that G-d is good and that all we receive from G-d is good, we transform ourselves.

If we insisted that the only good is that which is openly revealed to our intellect as good, then we have set ourselves up as gods. We have closed the system and bounded good according to our own dictates. We have left no room in the world for G-d, we want the world to operate according to our dictates, and we leave no room for the possibility that it operates according to higher dictates.

However, by trust in G-d that He is the source of all, and thus by definition all is good - we open up the world. We allow ourselves to be open to G-dliness. That ourselves, our situation, and our world operates according to G-dly dictates. And though we might not perceive the goodness of G-d's plan, we have trust that it indeed is good.

This change in our outlook is itself a change in our situation. This trust itself transforms us and makes us worthy.

This is what King David says in Psalm 55

Throw onto G-d your needs, and he will support you, he will never allow the righteous to fall.

By having an active positive trust in G-d, one changes one's situation and becomes worthy of all good things - even if we don't have the merits otherwise. Just having this trust is itself a merit which will provide us will all we need, and never let us fall.

Chapter 11 Being Honest in Business

This is a big one. And an important one. And a complicated one. So let's get started.

I got an email once from a coaching client asking if the Universe will care if she cheats, just a bit, on her taxes. To be honest, I was astounded by the question. How can cheating possibly be beneficial?

I'll get into the sources from the Torah and Talmud shortly, but first a personal story. I love cats. I moved into my college dorm (many years ago) and wanted to adopt a cat immediately, but the landlord didn't allow pets without the pet being an emotional support animal. I spoke to some upperclassmen, and they told me that plenty of people have pets and that it's not a big deal. My first thought was to take their word for it and adopt a cat without getting it authorized. I thought about it for a bit and realized that I would have to lie to the cat shelter, telling them that my landlord allows pets.

Oh common, you might say, it's just a little white lie; nobody will be hurt, you're not trying to make a profit or somehow take someone's money legitimately. True, but here's the big issue: lying is never good, no matter how small.

Here's what happened. A few weeks later, a water pipe burst in an apartment a few floors above me causing a major flood. Fifteen apartments had to leave, I was one of them, and go to a hotel for ten days. Now here's the thing. If I had a cat at the time, without the authorization, the school would not be responsible to either put me in a hotel that allows cats or put the cat up in a cat hotel, and either way it would be a trauma for the cat to move to a hotel and back just a few weeks after moving in with me. And then of course I could have got into trouble just for the fact that I had the cat to begin with. Any way you slice it, it would not have been a pleasant experience.

Another story I'd like to share is about a family. The mother was in the hospital, and needed a blood donation for post-surgery. She had a rare blood type, and the only match in the family was the 17-year-old son. The son offered the dad that he would just say that he's 18, forgot his ID at home, and if the dad would vouch for his son it was likely that the hospital would agree.

Being that the blood was not an immediate emergency, the father would not allow his son to lie and donate blood. Even though the son would be 18 in just a few months, the father saw this as lying and therefore there would be no blessing in this act.

The family drove home that day, and got into a car accident. The son was injured and loss a lot of blood. After getting to the hospital, the doctor told the father that if the son had lost just one more half-cup of blood, he would have surely died. Being that the average blood donation is a pint of blood, roughly two cups, the father realized right away that not lying and not donating blood for the mother had in effect saved the son's life.

What these and many other stories illustrate, is that lying is never helpful, at least not in the long term. And that is the most basic rule in Jewish law business; be truthful. We'll explore more examples of what exactly this means, but just remember the most important and basic concept, be truthful in business and bless your business.

The Importance of Being Honest in Business

First of all, the Torah and the Talmud's attitude towards financial success are quite positive. From this viewpoint, wealth enables one to help others. G-d blesses those who use their wealth to help the poor (Deuteronomy 15:10; Isaiah 1:17-19; Proverbs 19:17).

The Talmud (Talmud, Taanit 9) describes wealth as a reward from G-d. The verse (Proverbs 11:24), "There is one who scatters and yet is given more" is interpreted as referring to one who spends his money on the needy. Wealth is seen as "comely to the righteous and comely to the world" (Talmud, Avos 6:8), and affluent people who used their possessions to help others were respected by the Talmudic sages (Talmud, Eruvin 86).

A story (Babylonian Talmud, Taanis 9b) that supports this view is the following. Ulla was from Israel but quite frequently traveled to Babylonia. Once, while in Babylonia, Ulla saw dark clouds gathered in the heavens. Certain it would rain, he asked some people to help bring his belongings inside. When the rain did not come, he said, "Just as the Babylonians lie, so too do their rains lie." Ulla's statement again connects dishonesty in everyday affairs with a lack of rain. In Ulla's agrarian society a drought would devastate the economy. **The Talmudic solution to economic security is honesty in all dealings.**

The Talmud states the key to becoming wealthy is honesty in business (Talmud, Niddah 70b). This belief is noted in another tractate, "Heaven rewards people living in Israel who are strict about giving their tithes with great wealth" (Talmud, Shabbat 119). The Talmud exhorts the public to "Let your fellow's money be as precious to you as your own" (Talmud, Avot 2:12). This is another way of stressing the importance of integrity in business and other matters. The Talmud also believes a leader or administrator engaging only in honest and dependable service within the community is divinely rewarded with wealth (Talmud, Yuma 22b).

The Talmud also offers some practical advice on how to become wealthy, "Whoever inspects his property every day will find an istira (an ancient coin)" (Talmud, Chullin 105). An individual diligent in inspecting one's property not only saves money but discovers problems that need to be corrected. This is similar to the proverb, "A stitch in time saves nine."

The Talmud notes Rav's business advice to his son Aibu, which included the idea to "sell your wares while the sand is still on your feet" (Talmud, Pesachim 113) — do not procrastinate. The idea of diversification — dividing one's assets into thirds: 1/3 in land, 1/3 in business, and 1/3 kept liquid — is mentioned in the Talmud (Talmud, Baba Metzia 42). The Talmudists believed one who obtains wisdom will also become wealthy (Talmud, Baba Bathra 25). They understood the importance of education and knowledge in becoming wealthy.

The Talmud stresses the importance of honest work. Rav once told Rabbi Kahana: Flay a carcass in the street and earn a wage.

The following Talmudic statements further demonstrate the importance of honesty:

Rabbi Yehuda, in Talmud Baba Kama 30, says "One who wishes to become pious must be scrupulous in observing the laws dealing with damages and torts."

"The first question an individual is asked in the afterlife at the final judgment is: 'Were you honest in your business dealings?'" (Talmud, Shabbat 31).

Obeying the strict letter of the law is not enough. Jerusalem was destroyed, according to the Talmud, for not doing more than the law required (Talmud, Baba Metzia 30). The Talmud uses the term "the way of the pious" to describe the highest form of ethical behavior. This simply means that it's not always enough to do the bare minimum requirements. Sometimes, when you feel it's appropriate, go the extra mile.

There's a great series of story books called "The Maggid Speaks," "The Maggid's table," and others. In one of the stories, someone came to the editor of the series and told him that he has "an amazing story." In short, a man had bought a hat from a hat store in Brooklyn. A few weeks later he got a phone call from the store owner. The owner told him that the hat distributor had mistakenly charged the store too much for the last shipment, let's say it was 10% extra. After the distributor reimbursed the store for the mistake, the store owner was calling the customers who were charged an extra 10% and told them to come pick up their reimbursements. That was the story told to the book editor. His response? "Isn't it a shame, that that story is 'an amazing story?'"

In other words, that story should be the norm. But unfortunately, many people in that situation might just see the mistake and the fact that they got reimbursed by the distributor as a stroke of good luck and that's that. But the truth is, that sort of behavior is simply being honest in business and should be the norm. Take this story to heart. When you do the right thing, you shouldn't see it as an amazing story; it should be the norm. And as we've seen from so many sources from the Torah and Talmud, being honest in business is indeed the secret to wealth.

And lastly, let me just point out that these sources are really just the tip of the iceberg when it comes to Judaic sources about being honest in business and so on. For example, the Talmud talks about employer-employee relationships, lending and borrowing money, tithing, and so on. But I think that if I had to summarize all the various texts, I think it all comes down to common sense about being honest and following the law,

Not Flaunting Wealth

The Talmud frowns on the conspicuous display of excessive wealth as it can lead one to arrogance. A successful individual may come to believe "the might of [their] hand made them wealthy"(Deuteronomy 8: 11-18). This isn't to say that you shouldn't enjoy your wealth. As the Talmud says, three things expand the mind, a pleasant home, pleasant dishes (or simply *things*) and a pleasant spouse.

So, like with many things in life, the job is find the right balance. I like to drive a nice car, but not one too flashy. I found a good balance with the Honda Accord. It's slick, but it's not a BMW or Mercedes. It's low maintenance and fairly comfortable. Not that I'm a Honda salesperson, but my example is just to illustrate that you can strike a balance between not flaunting wealth and still enjoying my lifestyle.

You are created in His Image, therefore, you are a creator. You create with your mind. You prepare the tools to accept your desires with your actions. You enhance your mind with kindness. You enhance your tools with peace. A short powerful prayer: G-d, the good bring close, the bad make distant, and the good in Your eyes fulfill.

Part Two

In this Part, Part two, we'll discuss specific ways you can make requests and special techniques to use to enhance your manifestation powers.

Chapter 12 The Power of Words

In Jewish teachings, much is attributed to the power of words. The world was created by G-d with words, Moses split the red sea with words, and Joshua brought down the walls of Jericho with words, and many others. Of course, there are many examples of this in the Talmud and Kabbala.

We spoke above about thinking good thoughts. This is the next level. Basically, when you want something to happen, to get something, to discover something, simply declare it. "I will get the job!" or "This will work out for the best," or "I will find the perfect home," and so on.

A very famous example of this in the Talmud is about dreams. The Talmud says, "all dreams go after the mouth," meaning, that the way you interpret a dream will change the outcome of the dream. You see, dreams are considered a form of prophecy, albeit it's a one in sixty of a prophecy. But in earlier times, when people were less bogged down by world news, global economies, and other types of modern day stress, people were more attuned to the spiritual, and thus their dreams were more powerful. Either way, no matter how strong of a prophecy a specific dream may be, the interpretation, i.e. what will actually manifest, is what you or someone else says the dream means.

For yourself or others, when you either remember or hear about a dream, say something positive! "This means you will be rich!" is a common response. Or "The dream means you will live a long life!" is another.

As you can see from this example, the words we use to declare something are very strong.

So, how does this work as a practical matter? When you want to achieve or attract a specific outcome, simply state that you will get it. Then believe it, and then release it.

I think this is a good place to bring up the idea that while you and I are extremely powerful beings, who are capable of attracting major events into our lives and capable of changing the world, we are still not G-d Himself. This is important to remember because there truly are "large picture" reasons for us to have or not have certain things. That being said, even in those cases the Sages teach us that enough prayer will still effect change. We learn this from Moses, who wanted to enter the land of Israel after leading the Jewish people for 40 years. There were very specific reasons why G-d didn't want him to. So, Moses prayed for many days until G-d eventually told him to stop, because if he would keep praying then G-d would have to let him in, and that would interfere with the larger plans. Keep in mind though, that most of us are not Moses and don't have as large an impact on the rest of the world, so this concern of interfering with the larger picture is less of a concern.

This is also the main difference between the techniques in part one, which are about general ways to lift your energy, and the techniques in part two, which are about achieving or attracting specific goals. The difference is that G-d has a lot of good in store for us, but we need to be capable of accepting His abundance. The way to do that is by using the techniques in Part One. They will raise your energy and allow abundance in all areas into your life. But Part two is about specific goals, which may or may not be in store for us. These are harder to obtain, but of course still possible, and even a lot easier than you may have previously thought.

Back to specific outcomes. So, after you have declared what it is you want, and believe that it will come true, you need to release it. This idea comes from the Mishna in Pirkey Avot that says that when a person runs after, or pursues, or doesn't let go, of his pursuit of honor, the honor runs away from him. This is the idea that holding onto, i.e. obsessing over a specific goal or outcome will just push it away. Rather, hold onto an intention with the thought that you will be fine without it. This can be hard with really big goals, and sometimes even seem counterproductive. But the truth is that the more we're willing to let go of the outcome, even all the while taking action to make it happen, the faster it will manifest.

There are many techniques out there on how to let go. Some gurus recommend writing goals or desires on a little wooden stick and throwing it into a river. Others write their goals on a balloon and let go of the balloon, (although I read that that can cause damage to wildlife). My recommendation is based on Psalms 55, where King David says, "Throw onto G-d your needs, and he will support you, he will never allow the righteous to fall." In other words, simply declare, in words or just to yourself, that you are letting go of the goal, desire, intention, and letting G-d take care of it for you.

Again, this too does not mean for you to then sit back and not act. Rather, now that you have asked the Creator to assist, start listening to those inner voices that are telling exactly what actions to take.

You are created in His Image, therefore, you are a creator. You create with your mind. You prepare the tools to accept your desires with your actions. You enhance your mind with kindness. You enhance your tools with peace. A short powerful prayer: G-d, the good bring close, the bad make distant, and the good in Your eyes fulfill.

Chapter 13 North and South

The Talmud says that one who wants to earn more money, should face north, and one who wants to gain intelligence, should face south. This can simply be done by facing these directions while trying to attract these things, or even thinking about these directions. The Talmud explains why this is, which is simply based on the locations of various items in the original Temple in Jerusalem, but for our purposes all we need to know is that these directions are helpful in attracting these things, respectively.

Chapter 14 Less is More

This is quite a deep idea, but one very helpful when we can truly understand and practice it.

The old joke is that a man prays every day to G-d asking to win the lottery. "Please!" the man moans, "please let me win the lottery." Finally, after a year of praying, G-d gets fed up and responds to the man, "then buy a damn ticket!"

This joke is meant to illustrate the point that it's not enough to pray or hope for something, rather one must take action as well.

However, the joke and its message have a limitation. What the joke and its message assume is that the person's personal belief system was that the only way to win the lottery was to buy a ticket. Therefore, and rightfully so, in that case the man would need to buy a lottery ticket in order to win.

However, if the man had a higher level of belief, that G-d can provide anything to anyone, at any time, and in any way He wants to, then buying the ticket won't be necessary. The man can find the ticket on the street, someone could gift him the ticket, and so on. But here's the imperative question: does the person truly believe that G-d can let him win the lottery without buying a ticket? If the answer is yes, he need not buy a ticket, but if the answer is no, and it is no for many people, then that person would need to buy a ticket.

You see, G-d allows us to run our own personal worlds, in the sense that the amount of effort we need to put into something is in accordance to own true beliefs. If one really, deep down, believes that G-d can and will provide all one's needs, but that in order to receive abundance one needs to work for an hour a day, or for four hours a week, then that will be the amount of work that the person indeed needs to perform.

So, when it comes to playing the lottery, the more you play, the more you're actually showing G-d, or the Universe, that you believe that in order to win the lottery the Universe *needs* you to buy so many tickets. But here's the thing: the less you buy, the more you are showing G-d that you believe in Him and that He can provide you with what you want with only minimal effort.

Here's your challenge: Take some time to really think about how much effort you need to need to put into something for it to work. What level of belief are you at? This should take some serious thought. But after you think about for a while, challenge yourself to see if you can believe that G-d can provide for you, in abundance, with just a little bit less work. So let's say you think you need to work for 40 hours a week in order to live well. Can you imagine a case where you could be successful with only 38 hours a week? Or perhaps you invest in marketing $100 a week. Can you imagine being just as successful, or even more successful, with only $90 a week?

Try it and see what happens. If it works, that means you've raised your personal belief system. If not, that means you need to take more time and thought before you can actually lesson your effort and still be as successful.

This is indeed a deep and complex issue, so I urge you to use caution. The Talmud also says that one should not rely on miracles, because that is the level at which most people operate. So use caution and thought. Don't invest money you can't afford to lose and test your faith. Rather, use baby steps, intuition, faith, and common sense.

You are created in His Image, therefore, you are a creator. You create with your mind. You prepare the tools to accept your desires with your actions. You enhance your mind with kindness. You enhance your tools with peace. A short powerful prayer: G-d, the good bring close, the bad make distant, and the good in Your eyes fulfill.

Chapter 15 Peace

As we've mentioned in the mantra at the end of nine of the chapters, "You enhance your tools with peace."

What this means is simple. You could store toothpaste in a bag, but a better vessel is in a tube. You could put pickles in a paper bag, but a better vessel is in a glass jar.

Spiritual "substances" have vessels too. The spiritual "substance" of blessing and abundance, is peace. The more peace you have with others, the larger your vessel. On the other side, even if someone merits blessing, if their vessel isn't large enough to receive it they indeed will not.

Do whatever you can to make peace with others. The more harmoniously you live with others the larger your vessel will be to receive blessings. This is a simple fix to many problems one might have in life, albeit not always an easy one.

Thinking about it this way, you might be more inclined to not get into fights, to not continue feuds, to not instigate or add fuel to any existing fights.

Lastly, helping others find peace between them is a huge merit for you as well. And by enlarging their vessels of blessings you are also raising your own.

Chapter 16 Hole of a Needle

There is a very famous saying in Jewish thought: "Make an opening for me, the size of a needle hole, and I will open, for you, an opening the size of a hall."

What this means is that G-d is telling us that all we need to do is try. Recently I was talking with a client about problems he was having in his marriage. He was blaming everything on his wife and claimed that he was not at fault at all. I told him that even if he's not at fault, he needs to do something, anything, in an effort to make peace at home.

He called me a few weeks later to report on the situation. He knew that his wife hated when he left the toilet seat up, so he started making sure that he closed it. And that's all it took. He and his wife completely made up and were doing great. Sometimes, doing just a small little bit can make a huge difference.

Conclusion

As we come to the conclusion of this writing, I'd like to mention a few ideas. First of all, this writing, as it pertains to Jewish law of attraction and other techniques for acquiring ones wants and desires, is really the tip of the iceberg. However, I do believe that I touched on the most important ideas, such as being honest in business, striving for peace, being kind and considerate with others, and so on. But, if you'd ever like to expand on your general Jewish understandings, I'd recommend the books by Rabbi Aryeh Kaplan.

I'd like to recommend going over the book at least twice. Not just are there many important ideas, some of the chapters, such as chapters 7, 10, 11, and 14 have some very deep ideas and concepts; perhaps just one reading isn't enough to fully absorb them.

Please don't hesitate to reach out to me via email. I can't promise I'll respond, as my schedule can be quite hectic, but I will try. My email address is **rabbiabrahamloa@gmail.com**.

I can try to answer your questions, and I also offer coaching, prayers, cleanings, and meditations. Email me for more details.

I've been asked by clients to summarize the Jewish law of attraction. Not to compare myself with the great scholar and leader Hillel from the Talmudic era, but he was asked a similar question. The Talmud (Shabbat 31) tells us that a man came to Hillel, (born in year 110 before common era) and asked the sage to distil the Torah into one sentence, or, as the man put it, "teach me the whole Torah while I stand on one foot." Hillel elegantly replied, "What is hateful to you, do not do to your fellow: this is the whole Torah; the rest is the explanation; go and learn."

While Hillel offered the man the Golden Rule, he also admonished him to learn the rest of the Torah, meaning it's okay to summarize but it's not enough; you also need to learn sources.

When it comes to the law of attraction, the same applies. By being a good, decent person, one will attract their needs and desires. And when one does good for their fellow human beings, and acts to help them acquire their wishes, one enhances their own power of attraction. It all works so well in harmony. And just one last time for the road:

You are created in His Image, therefore, you are a creator. You create with your mind. You prepare the tools to accept your desires with your actions. You enhance your mind with kindness. You enhance your tools with peace. A short powerful prayer: G-d, the good bring close, the bad make distant, and the good in Your eyes fulfill.

Here's to your amazing attraction abilities!
Rabbi Haim

Made in United States
North Haven, CT
19 May 2022